A Short Introduction to Coaching Skills and the GROW Model.

Updated and revised

P.H. Davies

Available in Spanish

Una breve introducción a las Habilidades de Coaching y al Modelo GROW

Traducido del inglés por Nicolas Argentato
www.modernforeignlanguages.net

Contents

1 Introduction

The aim of this short book is to give an idea of what coaching is and to show how it can help people to change things in their lives they want to change. It explains the principles behind coaching and enlarges on some of the methodology that has been shown to work both in professional coaching and with individuals who self-coach. It aims to provide information that, hopefully, is useful to somebody considering embarking on a coaching course as well as for people who may be simply interested in the subject.

Coaching can, and does, make a positive difference to people. Coaching can help people make the necessary decisions and take the appropriate actions to achieve significant and sustainable improvements in their life. Improvements can be to do with health and wellbeing, business, work-life balance, relationships, career or any area they choose. Given a desire to change and a willingness to try, coaching can be successfully applied to almost all aspects of life.

Coaching can be quite challenging. The letting go of old, redundant thought patterns and behaviours and the creation of new ones can be hard work. Sometimes it is a little scary. If something has served well enough for the last twenty years, why not hang on to it for a bit longer? Like an old pair of comfortable shoes, habits are hard to discard.

As a coach, there is enormous satisfaction and pleasure in watching a person grow and achieve. To be invited to work with somebody is a privilege, but with this privilege comes responsibility. It is important to remember that, as a coach, we are dealing with people's lives. Change always creates consequences; it is not an isolated thing. Change alters the equilibrium in which people live and there are usually repercussions; hopefully all very positive ones. It is not something to be taken lightly, but this doesn't mean it can't be exciting and fun. To watch somebody do something that, a short time ago, they thought beyond them is a truly rewarding experience. To experience it yourself through your own self coaching skills is even better.

2   What is coaching?

People often begin by telling you what coaching is not. They may say that it is not like counselling or mentoring, nor is it the same as consultancy; but they sometimes struggle to give a clear definition of what it actually is.

There are similarities between coaching, counselling, mentoring and consultancy, of course. They all work towards the growth and development of an individual or group. They all facilitate choices in future behaviour and enable greater understanding of the recipient's current situation. They help people gain new skills and new ways of learning. It can improve or progress a particular situation by providing solutions to potentially difficult issues. They all share the mutual goal of helping people move forward. However, there are differences between the methodologies.

Coaching is a conversation between two people, the coach and the person being coached, the coachee, during which the coach guides, supports and facilitates the coachee's progress towards certain defined goals. The coachees alone decide their goals and the coach helps to find ways to achieve them. The important point is that each goal and each required action is identified and decided upon by the coachee not the coach. If everything was decided by the coach the interaction would no longer be coaching, it would be something more akin to mentoring or consultancy where solutions and action plans are suggested or even imposed from the outside.

In coaching, coachees decide what they want to achieve and then, with varying degrees of support from the coach, commit to a series of actions that will lead to achieving them. Decisions and actions are owned entirely by the coachee. This makes such decisions and actions very personal and because they are not being imposed or suggested by anybody else, they are far more likely to be successful and sustainable. The coach acts as a facilitator, ensuring that the coachee commits to a series of actions within an agreed time scale while fully understanding and owning the consequences of their actions.

Some textbook definitions of coaching are:

"Coaching is a way of unlocking a person's potential to maximize their own performance in whatever chosen field. It is helping them learn rather than teaching them". (John Whitmore, Coaching for Performance; GROWING Human Potential and Purpose: The Principles and Practice of Coaching and Leadership.)

Coaching is "a process that enables learning and development to occur and thus performance to improve. To be successful, a coach requires a knowledge and understanding of process as well as the variety of styles, skills and techniques that are appropriate to the context in which coaching takes place" (Eric Parsloe. The Manager as Coach and Mentor , Published by the Chartered Institute of Personnel & Development, 1999)

3   What do coaches actually do?

This is a record of an actual conversation.

"So what do coaches do?"

"They help people who feel stuck, who need a bit of help to move on from a particular set of circumstances......"

"No, I mean, what do coaches actually do?"

"They help people decide on a sustainable course of action that will bring about beneficial changes in......."

"No, listen, I walk into your office, tell you I want some coaching; what do you do? Wave a magic wand and sort out all my problems or what?"

"Oh, I see. Coaches ask a lot of questions, lots and lots of questions. They listen carefully to what you tell them and then they ask some more questions."

"Oh, I get it, they're just like the Fraud Squad!"

Coaches do ask a lot of questions; this is the fundamental basis of coaching. They also listen intently to the answers. These are not ordinary conversational questions like, "How's your mother?" Coaching questions are different; there is a whole chapter dedicated to them later.

We are not all the same.

Everybody is different, it is what makes people so fascinating. We should appreciate and celebrate this individuality and never let it get in the way of building rapport with a coachee no matter how strange we may think they are. As a coach, we must be prepared to use slightly different approaches in how we build a sound and lasting rapport with each person and this sometimes requires skills not too far removed from acting. Fortunately, most of us possess and exercise such skills in a natural and unselfconscious way, though these skills can be learnt and developed through practice. Rapport building skills are vitally important and will be discussed later.

Coaches are different too. There are many different approaches to coaching and no two coaches do things in exactly the same way. Given some clearly defined boundaries and rules there is no absolutely right or wrong way to coach, as long as it is done in a way appropriate to the needs and expectations of the coachee.

Is it ever right to tell a coachee what to do?

It all depends on your definition of coaching and the style of coaching you adopt.

Non-directive coaching is the style of coaching based entirely on asking open questions. An open question is one that cannot be answered with a simple yes or no. They are designed to help the coachee find their own answers and solutions, there is no advice given and hardly ever any suggestions made. Skilled questioning helps coachees gain clarity, think about what is possible, get rid of inconsistencies and take responsibility for their own actions. The coachee has complete ownership of all decisions and actions. This can create a strong sense of empowerment, boost confidence and encourage proactive behaviour.

Non-directive coaching cannot be rushed, it takes time. Supporters of this approach argue that as the imagination and creativity of the coachee are bound up in the process, the results are more far-reaching and sustainable than a directive style.

There is a continuum between directive and non-directive coaching, it does not have to be an either-or situation. Sometimes, giving coachees a gentle prod, or providing a piece of information that would be of value to them might be a good idea. For example, if we sense that they have gone up a blind alley or are heading in a direction that could possibly cause harm, it may be appropriate to ask them a few direct questions about their chosen path.

There are other times when we may be in possession of knowledge and information that they need but don't appear to be able to access. So, with their permission, we give it to them. They may be stuck or too exhausted to find it for themselves. Most times the coachee is happy to receive this, but not always, so we should always ask permission first.

We are talking about information, not advice. Advice is something totally different. Any advice we give is based on our knowledge and our past experiences filtered through the perspective of our own personal value system, not theirs.

If a coachee appears determinedly set on a course of action that we are convinced will lead to disaster, one way of dealing with it is not to tell them they're doomed, but to ask them to explain the reasoning for their actions, ask them to share the evidence on which the action is based and then to explore the likely consequences of each action.

Directive coaching

The rules are largely the same but the amount of information and suggestions provided by the coach is significantly greater and is closer to teaching than coaching. With directive coaching, coaches often set specific goal-oriented tasks as homework.

Some coachees prefer the directive approach because, in a way, it can be seen as the easier option. If they appear stuck, the coach is likely to tell them what to do. Their creative processes are not overly challenged and, believing that the coach knows best, they accept the suggestions and build them into their plan. One issue is that the coachees have little ownership of the agreed actions and, as a result, might commit less effort to actually following through. For example, if things start to go wrong, the plan can easily be dropped as it wasn't their idea to begin with.

In most situations, a skilful combination of both approaches can be used, provided the underlying principles and protocols are followed.

4 The GROW model

The GROW model of coaching has been tried and tested for a long time. It works.

GROW is an acronym: **G** = goals, **R** = reality, **O** = options, **W** = will.

G represents your GOALS. What do you want to happen? What do you want to achieve? What do you want to do or have?

R represents your REALITY. What is happening right now? What is going on in your world that is relevant and pertinent to the situation you want to change?

O represents your OPTIONS. What could you do? What have you tried? What would you like to try? What is possible?

W represents your WILL. What will you do? Not only what, but when will you do it?

This model of coaching can be applied very successfully whether we are coaching ourselves or when we are working with a coachee. We use appropriate questions to navigate through the processes of identifying goals, understanding fully the reality of the situation, exploring options and finally committing to a series of simple steps that will lead to realising these goals.

Coaches tend not to follow a script or a prescribed set of coaching questions; they develop the ability to formulate their own questions for each stage. However, it is helpful to have a series of illustrative questions at hand as part of a coaching toolkit. They can act as a prompt and to inspire the crafting of new and individual specific questions.

The GROW model is also not a strictly linear model. We do start with goals and end up with a series of stated intended actions, but we can revisit any of the grow stages as the conversation develops and evolves. Goals may change as well as options and possibilities; the sequence can be as cyclical as we wish provided we end up with a clear set of stated actions. The coachee should always be allowed the flexibility to revisit any part of the coaching session whenever they want.

5   G is for GOALS

Without clear-cut goals people tend to drift about in all sorts of directions. If they are adrift they are not in control of where they are heading. If they are not in control they are not shaping their own future, maybe somebody else is. Clear-cut goals are like compass bearings or a destination programmed into a GPS. Without these directional aids, a person may well know where they want to go to but are more likely to be side-tracked on the way.

A study at Yale University in the 1950's noted that only 3% of the graduating class had written down a set of goals for their future lives and careers. Twenty years later this 3% were found to be financially worth more than the other 97% put together. They also had better relationships and better health.

The Goals part of any coaching session is taken up with identifying what coachees wants to talk about (the topic) and then, through a series of questions, helping them to clarify what it is exactly they want to achieve. In other words, their goals. Without a goal, coaching cannot begin. Coachees cannot end up where they want to be if they don't know where they are going.

Words to actions.

A goal is both an end point and a starting point. The goal-setting process enables coachees to express and record their goals in words that they can turn into positive, relevant and empowering action steps. Things they need to do, not just talk about. These actions lead to the goal being achieved. With no goals there are no options or actions, so nothing changes. One could argue that goal-setting is the most important part of a coaching session.

Sometimes it is not easy. Many people do not have the faintest idea what they really want to achieve but they can tell you a great deal about what they don't want to do. Also, people are sometimes more likely to get what they think about rather than what they want. If when a person falls asleep they are thinking about all the things in their life they don't like or don't want to do, these negative ideas can sink into their subconscious and have an adverse effect on proactive thinking and creativity. This can impact on their decision-making process. With nothing positive and specific to aim for it is all too easy to just go round in circles.

Goal setting can break this cycle of negativity and create a positive, more proactive and action-oriented way of thinking. It is one of the most important parts of the coaching process. The job of the coach is to work with the coachee on creating well-crafted goals in order to make the process of change successful and sustainable.

6   Different types of goals.

Ongoing, daily goals.

These involve actions that have to be done every day. The goal may be to spend more time with one's family, so the specific action may be to leave work an hour earlier each day. Daily goals might be part of the ongoing plan, for example, to lose weight. Controlling what you eat is a daily occurrence leading to the achievement of the long-term goal. The end result is achieved daily and repeated on a daily basis to succeed with the long-term goal.

Short-term goals.

Can be achieved within a week to a month.

Medium term goals.

Take between a month and a year to achieve.

Long-term goals.

Take a year or more to achieve.

Medium and long-term goals involve a series of ongoing and short-term goals that act like stepping stones or signposts.

"Most people overestimate what they can do in a year and underestimate what they can do in a decade." (Tony Robbins. Giant Steps: Small Changes to Make a Big Difference)

Three rules about goal setting:

1 Goals must be congruent with coachees' values and sit easily with their beliefs. If coachees declare an intention of doing something which contravenes what they believe in, the goal is unlikely to be achieved.

2 Goals must be written down. The simple act of writing a goal helps to embed it in the coachee's consciousness and encourages commitment. A written goal acts as visible stimulus to action.

3 Goals must be precise. Precision is important. A goal such as, "I want to spend six hours each week working with my local conservation group," is more likely to be achieved than something vague like, "I want to do something for the environment."

An exercise in goal setting.

Find somewhere quiet where you won't be disturbed; somewhere you can't hear the phone or the TV or the kids playing. Think of five topics, five areas of your life in which you would like to make changes. They could be related to business, personal relationships, work-life balance, health or any area that is important to you. Write them down. Think of some good things you would really like to do or achieve in these areas, making sure what you choose fits in with what you believe in.

Write them down.

Here are some examples to get you started:

Wellbeing - I am overweight.

Work life balance - I work too hard.

Finances - I never have enough money.

Social life - I want to see my friends more frequently.

Activities/sport - I want to run a marathon.

Write your topics on a piece of paper using short sentences that are easy to remember. Choose one. Read it carefully and ask yourself the following questions.

How realistic is this topic?

If you had written that you want to become a billionaire within the next five years, then maybe you need to question how realistic you are.

How important is this topic to you right now?

If it is not really important there will be little compelling desire to achieve it.

How specific is this topic?

Topics that are specific are quite easily turned into goals. They imply a desire for change and often begin with the words - I want to... or I would like to...

Is your goal written as a positive statement?

This is very important. So important it deserves a few pages of its own.

Positive or negative.

Look back at your goals. Are they positive or negative statements?

Are they "moving away from" or "working towards" statements?

Positive + working towards = good.

Negative + working away from = not so good.

For example, "I do not want to be working in that office for much longer," is a negative, away from sort of goal. It starts with an, "I do not"; it says where you want to get away from but it does not say where you want to go to. How will you get there if you don't know where it is? You could rephrase it in the positive by saying, "I want to work from home, or I want to work for X,Y or Z." This is a working towards statement. Positive, working towards goals tend to produce better results by focusing on what you want to do and can do rather than what you don't want to do and can't do. You could make your goal a bit more specific and identify what type of work you would like to do at home. Get the idea?

Try this exercise on reframing negative goals.

Change these questions into positive questions and then see if you can create a proactive goal from them.

Why do people at work always dump stuff me?

This could be rephrased as, "What do I need to do create better outcomes at work?"

From which a specific proactive goal can be developed.

Try these.

Why can't I understand this issue?

Why are my writing skills so rubbish?

Why can I not see the answer to this question?

Why do people never pay attention to what I say?

Negative questions often produce negative answers and are hard to reframe into a positively stated goal. They do not stimulate new and different behaviours which, after all, is what coaching is all about. Rephrasing the question positively helps get rid of pre-programmed thinking and encourages new ideas. Changed thinking leads to changed behaviours which leads to changed lives.

What was it Einstein said? A true sign of madness is doing the same old thing again and again and expecting a different result each time.

Some more examples:

"I am overweight," can be rephrased as the goal, "I want to lose weight."

Whilst this is a perfectly valid goal it would be better phrased in a specific way.

"I want to reach my target weight of 125lb by my birthday."

This produces a target and a time in which to achieve it.

"I work too hard," can be changed into the goal, "I want to work fewer hours each week," or more precisely, "I want leave the office at 5pm every day."

"I never have enough money," could be rephrased as, "I want to create a good budgeting plan and stick to it."

To recap.

The topic is the thought or idea; the goal is the target you have created.

The goal needs to be worded in a positive way. The goal needs to be precise.

Back to you.

Look through the topics on your list.

If they are not written as positive goals, change them now.

Think about your reasons for writing them. If there are any items that aren't specific or realistic then either rewrite them or cross them off the list.

Arrange the remaining ones in order of importance. Keep the top five and discard the rest.

Define what success means to you in each of the items you have listed.

Will being successful in this area improve the quality of your life? If so, how?

For each of your goals, ask yourself if it fits your values. Then, take each goal in turn and make a to-do list stating what you are willing to do and what you will need to do to achieve it.

Include,

the people who can help you

the skills you might need to develop

the actions you need to take

what you need to learn

what you need to understand.

Look at your goals and decide which are

on-going goals that need daily input

short-term goals to achieve within a week to a month

medium-term goals to achieve within the next few months

long-term or life goals.

Congratulations. If you do all this, you will have achieved more in a couple of hours than most people will have done in a lifetime. Doesn't that make you feel ready to get on with things?

Now that you have a clear idea of what you want to do take yourself forward to the age of 90 and do the rocking chair test. Imagine thinking back over the wonderful life you designed for yourself. Visualise it, enjoy, fully associate with it.

How does that make you feel?

7 Good goals are SMART goals

S = specific

M = measurable

A = attainable

R = realistic and

T = timed, or set to a realistic timescale.

SMART goals are more likely to be achieved.

Specific goals are preferable to vague, generalised ones.

Specific goals are easier to work towards; you can see

the target. For example, the goal, "I want to do some

environmental work," is harder to work towards than

the more precise, "I want to create an educational

programme to teach energy efficiency within the home."

When a goal is sufficiently specific you should be able to

answer the following questions.

Who – who else other than you is involved?

What – what exactly do you want to achieve?

Where – where will all this take place?

When – is there a written time frame?

Which – what is needed to make it happen?

Why – what is the benefit or purpose of doing this?

If you can answer all of these clearly then you are well on your way.

Measurable goals should have clearly defined markers of success. If there is nothing measurable how will you know when you have achieved it?

Questions such as how much and how many can focus your mind.

How many hours will you do in the gym this week?

How much money will you put in your savings account each month?

How much weight will you lose this week?

With some imagination you can decide upon appropriate markers for almost anything.

Goals need to be attainable and appropriate. If they are too unrealistic they will be daunting. They could be broken down into smaller, attainable goals – stepping stones that are better suited for the present situation. Conversely, if the goal isn't challenging enough you will soon become bored, get insufficient reward and are quite likely give up.

A realistic goal is one that you are willing and able to work towards. This is a personal matter. You might be able to achieve it relatively quickly, but if you are unwilling to do so because it doesn't fit comfortably into your values and belief system, it isn't likely to happen. If it does happen, you mightn't be happy with the results and a conflict may develop. Values and beliefs will be discussed in detail later. If the goal is beyond your abilities it may be unrealistic in its present form so break it into smaller, easier steps. If it is still unattainable let it go.

A timed goal has target dates built into it. Without dates it would be insufficiently motivating and it would be easy to let things drift. People can get so carried away with long-term goals and dreams of retiring to a Caribbean island that they often forget to nail down the details of what they want to do today.

Embedding a goal

Choose your favourite goal from the list you made earlier. You are now going to plant it in your imagination.

Make sure your goal is written down and is very clear in your mind.

This exercise will embed both the goal and the consequences of achieving it in your subconscious. It is like a seed planted in your mind. If it is captured in your imagination you are likely to think about it more and, as a result, are more likely to actually do it.

Concentrate your mind on this goal, really focus.

Take yourself forward to a moment in time when you have achieved this goal and things are just as you want them to be. Think hard about this, strain yourself. It will help to clarify whether the goal is realistic and appropriate.

Have a good look around you in this imaginary future.

What do you notice in your mind that shows that you have achieved this goal?

Write it down.

Picture what you are doing that shows you have achieved this goal?

Write it down.

What are you hearing that tells you that you have achieved this goal?

Write it down.

What are you feeling that confirms you have achieved this goal?

Write it down.

What are you saying to yourself that tells you have achieved this goal?

Write it down.

Do you still feel happy about this goal?

If, after doing this exercise, the feelings associated with achieving this goal just don't sit comfortably, then in all probability the goal is not right for you at this time. If everything does feel good, then the goal is appropriate and so is much more likely to be achieved.

90% of success in achieving a goal is about the **WHY** and the motivational level and only **10%** about the **HOW** and the concrete tasks involved. If the why is right the how tends to follow on.

If everything so far is good, then great, carry on. If not, think about what is creating discomfort and change it. If everything feels right then the goal is beginning to send out roots in your subconscious.

When would you like to achieve this goal?

A timescale is essential. How long do you want to spend working towards this? If the size of the goal is so large that it requires a long time to achieve, it would be a good idea to break it down to a series of steps or shorter-term goals called journey goals. These smaller steps are easier to manage time wise but will lead to the achievement of the final goal. If you want to run marathons, you don't begin by doing twenty-six-mile training runs.

How challenging or exciting is it to achieve this goal?

If it isn't challenging enough, you may well lose interest. If it is too challenging or unrealistic you can break it down to achievable journey goals. An achievable goal for one person may be an impossible or daunting challenge for another. We are all different.

Measurement means movement. Is there a measurement you can use? Almost everything can be measured in some way. Things like weight loss, time management and money can be easily quantified. If there is a scale of measurement you can use then progress is easier to record and assess.

What areas do you have control or influence over?

List the people you may have to talk to or ask for help and advice in achieving this goal; the people you will need to work with, the skills you may need to develop, what you may have to learn or maybe unlearn.

Goal setting does make you think!

The act of doing all this mental activity will fine tune and modify your goal. Sometimes it can change it completely. Re-examine your goal; if it is still relevant, write it down and keep it somewhere you can see it every day. Looking at it every day will embed it deeper into your subconscious and you will soon start to do something about it.

8   Coaching questions.

Coaches do ask a lot of questions. So it is a good idea to talk about the kinds of questions that they ask and understand how they differ from the kind floating around in general conversation.

Why do coaches ask so many questions?

It is not because they are nosey.

It is because coaching questions are aimed at challenging coachees to think, to reflect and to use their responses to make proactive decisions. If framed well they require thought, a reasoned reply and effort on the part of the coachee. Good coaching questions are often not easy to answer, but act like a catalyst. They can generate the spark that allows coachees to find their own solutions and create a practical, realistic way forward.

Questions like, "How's your dog?" are usually just requesting information. Conversational questions are mostly chatting.

Coaches do not ask closed questions.

Any question that can be answered with a yes or a no is a closed question. They are best avoided. They tell you nothing and they don't make the coachee think. They almost encourage the opposite of reflection, a quick yes or no is easy.

An open question requires an answer of at least a sentence and some degree of thought.

An example of a closed question.

Did you do the task you agreed to in our last session? The answer could be yes, no, or the equivalent of mind your own business. If the answer is yes, you will have to ask another question to extract details. If the answer is no, coachees might begin to feel defensive and start justifying why they didn't act, or they could become evasive. Either way rapport could be threatened.

A better question.

What you have achieved since we last spoke? It is an open question which requires thought. It is positive in that is asks for achievements. Even if the coachee hadn't fully completed the task he or she can tell you about the parts they did achieve.

If they hadn't done anything at all you could ask them to explain their inaction.

Do not use the W word!

Coaching questions should never begin with **WHY.**

Why is a powerful little word, it can sound rather accusatory. Why did you do that? Why didn't you do as you promised? Why is often linked to memories of situations where we have had to explain ourselves. It is often associated with providing reasons and excuses for when things have gone wrong rather than eliciting carefully thought out responses. If you really need to know why, ask for the reasons behind an action, e.g. what are the reason you did that?

Closed question – Did you go to the gym this week?

Open question - How are you progressing with your keep fit regime?

Closed question – Have you read the article I sent you?

Open question – What did you think of the article I sent you?

An exercise on Open and Closed Questions.

Rephrase these closed questions to make them open questions.

Is there anything stopping you from doing this?

Are you happy with that?

Does this take place frequently?

Is there anything else?

Has this coaching session been useful to you?

Do you have the resources to get through this?

Think up as many closed questions as you can; questions that illicit a one-word answer or a shrug. Make a note of the words that commonly start closed questions. Then do the same for open questions; ones that encourage an open reasoned response. Notice the difference?

To recap

Open questions make the coachee think and, as a result, produce better answers. Better answers lead to better actions. We can try to spend a day avoiding all closed questions and asking only open ones. People we speak to subconsciously become aware that we are really listening to them and want to understand them. It helps build rapport and they will appreciate it.

There are rules about asking coaching questions.
If you aren't fond of rules let's call them strongly worded recommendations.

Before you start practicing your coaching skills on somebody explain that you are going to ask lots of questions. Explain why asking questions is so important and reassure that there are no right or wrong answers just honest ones.

Make sure you word the questions carefully so that the meaning is clear.
Be patient with coachees.
Do not jump straight in after asking a question, the coachee may need several minutes to think about the answer. You do not have to fill the silence.

Do not ask complex or multiple questions. Keep them short and simple.

Always be encouraging and positive in acknowledging their answers.

Listen carefully to their answers and think before you respond.

Do not assume you know what the coachee is going to say.

Do not assume the coachee's first answer is the complete picture or even an honest picture.

Carefully and skilfully probe to get extra information if more depth is needed.

In sensitive areas do ask permission to question.

Do not wander off track. No matter how fascinating the coachee is, keep them on task. Gently and politely.

Do not ask leading questions. Leading questions suggest an answer in their wording. It is often the answer you want to hear not the one they want to give. For example, "Do you have problems with your boss?" This subtly suggests that there may be issues the coachee wants to talk about. It is also a closed question. A non-leading way of getting the same information is to say, "Would you like to tell me about your relationship with your boss." Whilst this is a closed question it demonstrates sensitivity in asking permission to discuss a relationship and if probed appropriately may lead on to useful coaching conversation.

Do not be afraid of trying. Just as there are no definitive right and wrong answers, there are no definitive right or wrong questions.

Use a variety of questioning techniques.

Maintain rapport with the coachee at all times even if the questioning gets a little tricky in places.

Practice all this on your friends and family.

Remember, better questions make for better answers.

Build up a toolkit full of questions that work for you.

9   Rapport.

Before we move on to the Reality part of the GROW model we really need to talk about another **R** - Rapport. Coaching without establishing rapport is not really possible.

Rapport is defined as: *a harmonious or sympathetic connection or relation. Or the ability to enter a person's model of the world so that you can give them the feeling of being totally understood.*

The key word here is **understood**.

People may tell you things that they have never told anybody else, possibly not even themselves. This will happen only if they trust you.

People tend to like and trust people who are similar to themselves. The art of developing rapport is to find a way of presenting yourself as being very much like the person you are talking to. Most people can do this naturally without ever having to think about it, it is an innate skill.

Some of the things that have been shown to quickly establish rapport with strangers can, on first reading, make us hesitate and think, "I'm not doing that." But when we step back and reflect, it is what we do all the time; every time we meet friends or interact with family. It is such a natural process we do it without being aware of it. However, coaches need to work at developing a rapport and so have to practice the skills necessary to do so.

Matching and Mirroring.

Watch two old friends relaxing in a café or a pub. They sometimes appear like mirror images of each other in terms of their facial expressions, their posture, their movements. When one leans back, the other usually will, when one picks up their drink, so does the other, when one looks wistful so will the other. It is a natural and unconscious aspect of personal interaction. It is what friends do.

If we can do the same with our coachees we are off to a good start, it will subconsciously suggest to them that we are a friend.

Mirror the coachee's body movements, position and tonality.

This takes quite a lot of practice to get it right. If they change body position, we wait a few seconds then we change ours to match theirs.

It is very important that this is not done in a clumsy, obvious manner or in a way that is culturally inappropriate.

If they use hand gestures when they speak we use the same hand gestures ourselves but only when it is our turn to talk and without making it obvious. We avoid inappropriate gestures. We match their facial expressions immediately. If they raise their eyebrows, we raise ours. When they nod their head, we nod ours immediately to show that we agree with what they are saying.

We must never try to copy an accent or any speech patterns that are distinct to that individual, for example, a lisp or a stammer, as that would be disrespectful. There is a fine line between mimicking and being insensitive and disrespectful. .

Do they talk loudly or quietly? We should try to talk at their volume level at all times, unless they are yelling. We mimic the depth of their voice if we can do it without sounding strange. We match the speed of their speech, the length of their pauses.

This is not as difficult as it sounds. It requires very good listening skills. If we practice, we will find that both our listening and acting skills improve rapidly.

Repeat and approve.

This is simple but effective. After they speak, we give a very brief synopsis of what they just said and then give our approval by saying something like 'excellent, great, wonderful, that's exciting'. This shows that we are indeed listening.

Assume you already have rapport.

We should talk to the person as if they're somebody we already know well and we completely trust, and who completely trusts us. If we do this, we will send out subconscious signals encouraging the other person to view us the same way.

For some people, matching and mirroring can seem a daunting challenge. It does take practice, so go ahead and practice. Most of us have these skills already and use them every single day.

10   R is for REALITY

This is where we talk about what is happening in the coachee's world, where we learn about the reality of their situation. This is where we begin to get to know them as we explore the things they want to change, what they want to keep, what they want to improve. This is sometimes the easiest phase to work through, particularly if it is primarily concerned with business or work. We may occasionally ask them how they feel about a particular situation, but most information provided is factual, organisational or numerical. Unless we feel that the coachee is hiding something from us or themselves, or that there are some deeper issues involved, the questioning tends to be straightforward and largely fact-finding.

The reality phase of the coaching session can also sometimes be the most difficult phase to work through. The coachee may have to face up to past and present failures, current difficulties and issues, problems with staff, money, family and friends and then tell us about it all. It demands a lot of trust on their part.

As a coach, our duty is to maintain our own positive attitude, to encourage positive, proactive thinking on the part of the coachee and to steer well away from simply providing a sympathetic ear and giving advice.

There will be times when we are told things we might not want to hear. These situations call for very careful handling. If it is important for a coachee to tell us something, we should respect their wishes and listen if it is relevant, appropriate and time allows.

Sometimes we may sense that the coachee is holding back, not telling us the whole story or deliberately missing out certain key facts. Do we carefully question and encourage the coachee to talk about things that we believe are necessary to know in order to make progress, or do we skirt round the subject and move on? This also calls for careful judgement on our part.

If we genuinely believe that our coachee requires some other form of professional help with emotional or psychological issues, for example, maybe if we were appropriately qualified in the relevant field, we could ask their permission to talk to them at another time. If we don't feel absolutely confident in our knowledge and abilities, we should stay well clear. We can do our best to help them but only by following strict coaching guidelines. If, after a number of sessions, we feel we are achieving nothing or that the continued association is doing them, or us, no good then we can tactfully suggest they may be better served in ways other than coaching.

So what do we do now?

We ask questions of course.

We reiterate the coachee's stated goal then ask the kinds of questions listed below.

What is happening right now that tells you that you have a problem?

What is missing in your present situation that you would like to have?

What is happening that is good, that you would like to keep?

What obstacles are preventing you from moving forward?

What have you done so far to improve things?

What were the results?

How far have you come?

How much further do you have to go?

What resources do you already have to help you reach your goal? Such as skills, qualifications, money, family support and so on.

What resources do you need? Where will you get them?

If there is somebody else involved what have they done to help you move on?

What will they have to do to help you move on?

How achievable is your goal?

How achievable is your goal with the group of people involved?

What behaviours do you have to change in order to achieve this goal?

Sometimes, after a series of questions the goal changes slightly or evolves into something completely different. Ask: -

Has your goal changed in any way? If it has, create a new one and write it down.

The Reality phase can be straightforward and simple but sometimes the information the coachee provides is confusing. Further questioning and requests for clarification may be needed. Very occasionally it can be like opening Pandora's Box. With self-coaching it can also be difficult to be totally honest with ourselves.

11 Self-fulfilling prophecies.

If we think we are poor at something then we will most likely behave as if we are actually poor at it. This happens even if deep down we know we are not really that bad at it and have no evidence to back up our reasons for thinking so. We have created a thought pattern and have trained ourselves into believing it is fact. It is like a self-fulfilling prophecy.

If we think it is always our fault when things don't work, others will start to believe that too. We may believe that we are frequently responsible for certain tasks going wrong or situations not working out well at work or at home. There may be absolutely no evidence to back this up other than a natural tendency to blame ourselves for everything. Negativity and a sense of futility can creep in. Because we suspect what we are trying to do isn't going to work we may not give it our best shot, and so when it does go wrong it proves yet again that it really is our fault. So let's not bother in the first place.

Both of these are examples of self-limiting beliefs.

Self-limiting beliefs will be covered later. They also illustrate the harm caused by negative thinking. Positive thinking is not going to change the world. But it might change a little bit of our world sufficiently to help us break out of a negative, non-achieving spiral.

As I lay me down to sleep.

If, just as we are falling asleep, we think about something negative, or an obstacle or a problem, the thought can stay in our subconscious mind all night, working away at undermining our confidence and our belief in ourselves. So, when we wake up at three in the morning the thoughts zinging round our head tend not to make us chuckle in the pleasurable anticipation of the day to come.

We are more likely wake up with that negative thought still there, but it will have morphed into the equivalent of a handful of sand thrown into our creativity processes. Negative thinking can kill originality and proactivity and it gets in the way of the thought processes associated with the achievement of something good.

Try this.

Just before you go to sleep you take in a deep, slow breath through your nose, hold it two seconds then exhale slowly through your mouth. Do this ten times in a row. Oxygenating the brain is good for us and the breathing helps in shifting stuck thoughts.

Think of something you did well recently, something that you are pleased with. Whether it is a big thing or a small thing, at work or home, no matter, just think of something you did that made you feel happy. Relive doing this thing.

Take five more breaths in and out, then think about the following.

What are you feeling when you relive doing this thing?

What can you hear, what can you see?

Hold those images and feelings in your head.

Say something positive and optimistic such as "I did that really well; next time I will be even better."

Say this sentence to yourself five times before falling asleep. You could well wake up in the morning feeling better. This may not happen immediately so you need to stick with it and practice every night.

Our minds often follow our bodies.

Sports people know that body memory is as important as brain memory. Watch any professional tennis player before they serve. They go through precise, repetitive movements that are designed to synchronise their muscular-skeletal memory with that of their brain, so what follows is a well-rehearsed, successful serve. Their bodies remember the posture and movements and so become primed for success before the action even takes place. Our bodies and our behaviours influence our mind, which leads on to acting as if.

Acting as if.

This is based on Aristotle's premise that if we act as if we are virtuous we will eventually become virtuous. If we behave in a certain way our state of mind often copies our body mood. It is called acting as if.

Whatever we want to achieve, we just think how we would behave if we had just achieved it. Then we act like it. We do the strutting, the secret inner smile, or whatever it is that we do. We do it again and again and our mind-set will soon become more positive and follow the change in our bodily behaviour.

It could be something to do with sport, work, relationships, wherever. We can set ourselves lots of daily imaginary successes and act out our celebrations accordingly.

Avoid negative company. Negative people should be avoided, they can drag you down and minimise your hopes and dreams. If you cannot get away from them, you must find a way to try to not to let them get through to you.

Do something good for somebody.
It will make you feel better than the recipient. Make a habit of it. You may have to be a little selective about the recipients of these acts; pressing bouquets of

flowers into the arms of passing strangers could be open to misinterpretation.

A random act of generosity.

Give money to strangers. What, are you mad? Some people do this to help them feel good about themselves and their place in the world.

The following is true. It involves the pairing of anonymous giving and totally random receiving. I know somebody who goes to a public library once a week, chooses a book at random, places a £10 note in it and returns it to the shelf. The cosmos decides who gets it. Statistically that is not correct, a lot depends on whether the book is a teenage vampire tale or a hefty work on Quantum Mechanics.

Donating to charity or volunteering one's time are the equivalent However you approach it, practicing random acts of kindness and generosity, however small, help you to feel better about yourself and help to create a virtuous cycle in life.

12   Options

Back to the GROW model. The options phase is where we discover a great deal about coachees. This is where their personality shows through most clearly, where we help them uncover their creativity, flair and imagination. This is where their history surfaces and where their values and beliefs will be expressed through what they say is possible or impossible. Limiting beliefs will have to be challenged as well as timidity, There is no right or wrong way of achieving our goals only the appropriate way that is effective for us. What may seem meticulously painstaking and glacially slow to some might appear like a headlong rush to others. Whatever our personal opinions are we have to accept and appreciate the differences.

We all have different skills, resources and mind-sets. Somebody with compromised health and limited mobility may have to spend such a high percentage of their financial resources on care provision that there is not much left over for boldly going where nobody has gone before.   However, we all have options regardless of our personal situation and level of resource.

 A few of the questions we might ask during the Options phase are listed below. There are thousands of possibilities but these will do to begin with. They are all about getting the coachee to think about their first steps.

Try these on yourself.

Go back to the goal setting exercise you did earlier, write out your main goal on a piece of paper and then ask yourself these questions. As always, write your answers down.

What could you do right now to move yourself forward just one small step?

What else could you do?

If you were not answerable to anybody, were completely autonomous, what else could you do?

Supposing you had unlimited funds and resources what would you do?

If you could focus all your time on one thing what would you do?

If there were no consequences what would you do?

Look back at the list of options you have written. Read them carefully and see if they generate a few more ideas. If they do, write them down.

Choose one option, the one that can move you forward just one step. It can be the cheapest or the easiest or the most pleasurable one to do.

If you do this one thing will it really move you forward? If no, choose another. If yes, stay with it.

What is the benefit to you of doing this one thing?

There has to be a benefit, otherwise why do it? Doing it may help you learn something, change your thinking about something, reduce your stress level, make you happier. When you know the answer write it down.

What is the purpose of asking Options questions?

To help stimulate the imagination and creativity of the coachee to think of ways round obstacles or ways to avoid the obstacles altogether. To help them create sustainable actions that lead to achieving their stated goal.

It is here you can see the coachee come alive as it dawns on them that, 'Yes, I can do this,' as opposed to, 'no, I can't.'

13   Beliefs and values.

The options phase is where these may be most evident and have the greatest influence. The dictionary says a belief is: A principle accepted as true or real without proof. An opinion, a conviction.

These may be religious, political, economic, philosophical, or of any shape, size and colour you can think of. We all have them; some make sense to others, some don't. If we feel that there may be a potential incompatibility between a person's stated goal and their beliefs, we can ask simple questions such as: -

How does this goal fit in with your beliefs?
How does achieving this goal improve your life?
How does achieving this goal improve the lives of the other people involved?

Some coachees will have already thought this through for themselves and are likely to be happy with this. A few people may not actually be aware of what their deep seated values are and others may be prepared to bury them for the sake of business, adopting the

Groucho Marx philosophy, 'Those are my principles and if you don't like them, I have others.'

It may be difficult to get people to talk about what they believe in, they may feel it is nobody's business but their own. However, as a coach we may need to explore this area, and if necessary, explain why it is so important to ask these kinds of questions. In doing so it is essential to explain that we are not making any judgements about anybody's beliefs and values.

Limiting beliefs.

We are all products of our own personal life history. When we are growing up, going to school, meeting new people we are forever being told things about ourselves. Sometimes what people say is positive but sometimes it is not. People can be very free with their criticism and unfortunately some of it sticks.

We can sometimes form ideas and beliefs about ourselves that are just reflections of other people's opinion. They need not necessarily be accurate and often have no evidence to back them up other than that we happen to believe them. We have been told these things so often that they have sunk deep into our subconscious and so must be true.

Somebody who has received constant criticism, been told that they are useless at something enough times will come to believe it. Even if there is not a shred of evidence. Being reminded of all the things you cannot do, what you are no good at can make the world a rather restricted place.

These beliefs are mostly formed in childhood or adolescence but they can last a lifetime and have a profound influence on the course of our lives. We collect and store a great deal of negative feedback we experience while growing up. Being ridiculed by being called stupid or clumsy tends not to be forgotten. It is filed away in the back of our minds only to emerge as an absolute fact when we are adults.

We grow in the belief we are clumsy and we are sometimes stupid and therefore incapable of understanding maths/foreign languages/logic/the offside rule in rugby/whatever. By the time we are adults these beliefs are often unshakable because they have been reinforced by both ourselves and others. This is the negative side of *acting as if.* For some people it is a safe place to live,

These beliefs are so deeply held they have the power to create, or help, or hinder or even destroy any possible course of action. Many of our ideas, expectations and deeds are influenced by such beliefs. What a person says or thinks they can and cannot do is informative.

Anthony Robbins states that the most important opinion a person will ever hold is the one they hold about themselves.

In her book "Developing a Growth Mindset," Carol Dweik talks about "the power of yet" and how the use of that one little word can be life changing. When a child or an adult says, " I can't do that" and stops there, they are saying " I can't, and I won't ever learn that." When they say, "I can't do it YET," they are indicating they are open to learning, open to development and improvement. Helping coachees to develop a growth mindset and to believe that they can change limiting beliefs is central to the coach's purpose.

Limiting beliefs are…. well, limiting.

If we believe we cannot do something we will often not attempt it. The more limiting beliefs we possess the less we are prepared to try and the breadth and quality of our lives can be adversely affected.

We will sometimes come across a coachee who has so many limiting beliefs that they do not want to ever attempt anything new, it is too scary. They believe that whatever the task is it is beyond them. For such people there is safety in inaction.

Their goal setting won't move them out of their comfort zone and the options they consider are often at too low a level and too safe to achieve much.

Such people need to be encouraged, supported and occasionally challenged. We need to be careful, there is a fine line between appropriately challenging somebody's self-imposed limitations and scaring them off.

A non-challenging way to help a coachee who is unable or unwilling to see a way forward is to pose a two-part question beginning with what if.
What-if questions are a good way to help somebody who feels they are unable to do anything to move forward and unable to come up with any options.
The what if part can temporarily suspend their limiting belief, even if just for a moment. The follow-up part of the question briefly allows them to be creative and imaginative. Even if it is just for a moment it may be enough to allow a glimmer of self-belief.

For example
With somebody who consistently says, "I could never do anything like X, we could ask: -
"What if you had all the resources you needed to do it, what would you do?"
"What if you knew with certainty that you could not fail, what would you do?"

"What if there were absolutely no consequences, what would you do?"

The **what if** allows a temporary suspension of disbelief in their own abilities. Conversely, you could say it temporarily suspends belief in their inabilities. It removes the fear from the challenge long enough for them to answer the question before the fear creeps back in. They don't just respond to the fear created by their negative belief.

Remove the fear then ask the question.
If a coachee persists in saying that they are not able to do X or have the skills to do Y or are rubbish at Z: -
Ask for the evidence they have to back up these statements.
Ask who told them so and how long ago it was.
Ask the coachee to rephrase their statements in a positive manner.
If they say: -"I am rubbish at maths," they can rephrase it as a goal such as, "I want to improve my maths skills."

"I would never be able to talk to a room full of people", can be rephrased, "I want to gain confidence in talking to groups".

"I always get things wrong in the office," can be challenged by simply asking, "Always? Or, "How does getting one or two things wrong in the past mean that you will always continue to get things wrong in the future?" Or, "Tell me about the last ten things you got wrong."

"I've tried absolutely everything and nothing works." Ask them to tell you about the last five things they tried. There are thousands of possible questions and many ways to rephrase negative statements. Persistence and patience will pay off.

Occasionally you meet levels of resistance that need a bit more work. If they are unwilling or unable to come up with any options they may rationalize their situation and make excuses for not doing anything to improve it. If the coachee is still resisting coming up with new ideas despite telling you that they are very unhappy about their present situation a more challenging type of question may be appropriate.

A question that touches upon their concept of free will.

Challenge them.

Ask them things like: -

What is holding you back from attempting your goal?

What are you getting out of being in this situation?

There must be some form of payback otherwise they wouldn't still be in it. Sometimes it is negative payback; staying put is less frightening than trying to change, so the payback is reduced fear.

What is in it for you?

This is another way of asking the same question.

What is the reason you are in this place/situation?

What are the reasons you are behaving in this way?

There is a fine balance between persisting until you get an answer and pushing the coachee too far. It can be difficult for somebody to be totally honest particularly if they are in a difficult and painful place; it may well be upsetting for them to talk about it. Gentle persistence can pay off, but if the coachee is showing signs of becoming upset or resistant, park the subject and find a different way of talking about it. .

If they are able to talk about things get them to imagine a future where all their goals are achieved. Then together find ways to get round the obstacle or objections they raised to taking the first steps.

If they are being particularly stubborn or resistant, you sometimes have to take them to uncomfortable places. It is not something to do lightly. If a person insists that they want change but are constantly unable to come up with any realistic options, or they are forever failing to complete the tasks they said they would, you could try the following.

Take them to the future. Ask them to visualise themselves in two or three years, where they have the same issues, the same difficulties and problems, where absolutely nothing has changed for the better.

Ask them how it feels to have all the same issues as now but magnified by the passing years.

Visualising a future that is bleak and dismal can sometime be the catalyst that makes them act.

Now we bring them back.

If you do take them to dark and dismal places you must make sure you bring them back to a bright cheerful one. You can get them to do the same exercise, but this time imagining all the good things in place as a result of achieving their goals. Asking them to compare the two places can be a significant catalyst. Then help them set goals and discuss ways to get there.

It is the **pain pleasure power** sequence that really helps motivation.

14   W is for WILL and WHEN

Basically the **W** phase covers who will do what, when, who with, how and what is needed in order to do it. It follows on from the options phase where the coachee decides what he or she can do, now they nail it down into what they will do. Coaching is an evolutionary process that starts with I would like to, moves through I can do, then on to I will do and ends up with I have done. You won't reach I have done unless the W phase is properly handled. The W phase is all to do with action. It is the time to get busy.

These are the kinds of W questions you may ask.
What are you going to do? List all the actions you have to do to complete the thing you have selected.
How will these actions meet your main goal?
When are you going to take these actions? What is the time scale?
How long do you think that this list of actions will take you? Can you work out possible time scales for each action?

Should anybody else be involved in this list of actions you have chosen to do? If yes, what do you want this person to do?

When will you tell him or her?

Who else should know that you will be doing these things?

What obstacles or barriers could get in the way of you taking the first step?

How likely will this obstacle stop you?

What can you do to make your first step more achievable? It may mean slight changes to your stated first step.

Everything needs to be written down with specified dates and times for each agreed action. "Sometime next week," will not do. If it is not in the diary it is not likely to be done.

This is the case whether you are talking about short term, long term or journey goals. Whatever needs to be done between now and the next coaching session has to be given a date and a time.

Timing is vital for commitment; when will they actually start, what day, what time and what place? Then they write it down and commit to doing it. They should place a copy of their to-do list on the fridge door or somewhere in plain view where they can see it every day.

How strong is your commitment?

Once a series of actions has been agreed and recorded it is a good idea to check how likely it is they will be carried out. Ask the coachee about their commitment level. Ask, "On a scale of 1 - 10 how likely is it that you will complete this action?"

If the answer is 7 or lower think of ways to increase it? Research shows that commitment levels of 7 and below are not likely to result in success.

Homework.

It is always a good idea to set the coachee some homework that goes above and beyond the series of actions they have agreed to in the **W** phase.

This could be a promise to take some time off, to go to the cinema, to read the book that has been sitting next to the bed for six months, to do something unrelated to work, to do something that maybe will help them holistically.

Or it could be directly related to their goals. If you feel there is an area that is being neglected or avoided for whatever reason you could ask the coachee to think about the issue at hand and talk about it next time you meet; or email some answers to you before the next session, some people prefer broaching difficult subjects by email rather than talking face to face.

In the follow up session
They can tell you all about what they did, what they achieved and maybe what they didn't do. It is important to praise their achievements and encourage further action. It is equally important to find out what they didn't achieve and discover the reasons. Remember to avoid the Why word.

If the reason they did not do what they said is simply time pressure then the goal could be broken into a series of journey goals that require smaller, more easily achieved action steps. It could have been a bad week where unexpected problems arose.

If they repeatedly do not achieve or even attempt their stated actions, then you will have to find an appropriate way of challenging them.

"What are the reasons you chose not to......?"

"What are you holding on to?"

"What is stopping you...?"

Maybe you could revisit challenging type questions outlined in the Options section.

People come to coaching for a variety of reasons. Most are to do with wanting to move forward and improving certain aspects of their life. Such people tend to be committed and will try, in varying degrees, to do as they promised. Others may have been bullied into coming by a spouse, partner, boss or whoever and are rather resentful of the whole process. Others come out of curiosity and have little genuine desire to change. Some are serial recipients of whatever therapy their peer group is into at the moment.

You may reach a stage where you know there is very little point in the coachee continuing with coaching So, it is your duty to the coachee and to yourself to tell them, positively and clearly, that you have gone as far as is possible together.

15 Staying in control.

Some people may refuse to answer certain questions. They may be evasive and skirt around particular issues. Others may appear unable to stop talking. They may go on at great length or fly off on totally irrelevant tangents.

While everybody should be given the time to talk and explain things it is important to keep them on task. Or, if they are being reticent, to challenge them about it. A thirty-minute digression on reef fish of the Caribbean may be fascinating but it wastes precious time and leads nowhere. Similarly, a session producing little more than grunts and head shakes is equally useless. If the coachee fully understands the process and what is expected from him or her then things tend to progress smoothly. If you, as the coach, follow the following ground rules then things should progress well.

Some valuable rules for a coaching session.

Ensure that the coachee understands what coaching is and that you are not going to provide them solutions to their problems. They will do that themselves.

Emphasise that coaching is not simply a conversation it requires actions.

Talk through any queries and concerns that the coachee may have.

Explain that coaches ask questions and that there are no right or wrong answers.

Set the parameters, discuss and agree the expectations of both coach and coachee.

Set clear session goals. Without these the session can end up spiralling out of control.

Agree a way to handle long silences. Find and agree a way for the coachee letting you know that they are still thinking and need more time to answer or that they are stuck and need a prompt.
Agree the best way to do that prompt? If they are still thinking and you interrupt them they will not be pleased.

Agree a way of the coachee telling you to stop if you stray into an area that they are not yet ready to talk about or do not feel comfortable with.

Likewise, if they are not happy with something you say or do.

Assure them that all conversations are totally confidential.

Avoid peripheral issues. Explain that lengthy personal digressions use up session time so less can be achieved.

One way of helping them keep on task is to say something like: -

Can we pause for a moment; how does this relate to the topic or issue?

Can I stop you for a moment; you began talking about XXXXXX can I bring you back to that.

Can I stop you there? We only have a few minutes left and I want you to decide on which options you want to pursue.

Can I stop you there? Perhaps we can come back to that during our next session.
Or more directly, "Would you like to come back to that later?"
Or even more directly, "We will come back to that issue in a moment".

Moving on statements are useful, for example "As fascinating as that is I would like to ask you about....."
Time warnings, for example, "As we have got only 10 minutes left how can we bring this session to a satisfactory conclusion?"

Use the Parking Lot.
A Parking Lot is somewhere to park a conversation that is going nowhere or that is a digression or smokescreen. Maybe it is one that needs to be examined in detail

some other time. Explain that topics placed in the parking lot are not lost forever just temporarily put on hold.

If you feel the coachee is losing interest tell them what each question is about before you ask it. It can re-engage them if they know why you are asking things.

Evading the question. A good approach would be: I understand you do not want to talk about this. That's fine, we can focus on other things. But first tell me the reason you don't want to talk about this. Answering this question will sometimes remove further avoidance.

There are times when things don't go to plan. It happens quite a lot. It is how we deal with situations that teaches and develops us most. It may lead to positive learning experiences.

Feedback.

It is important to get feedback, not just in coaching but in all sorts of situations. Feedback informs us about what we are doing well and about areas that need improvement. This applies whether you are coaching paying clients, practicing with friends and family or even coaching yourself. If you are self-coaching ask yourself how it went, which parts were good and which parts need improvement. Listen to the answers; you will know if they are truthful.

Sometimes it is difficult to ask others for feedback on your performance. You may be a bit reticent about asking 'How was it for you?' Suitable alternatives might be, 'How did you feel our session went?' or 'What was worthwhile about our session?' Or, 'What can I do differently next time to make it better for you?'

Asking for feedback is the only way we can gauge whether our direction and approach is appropriate. If the feedback shows that we are on course then we carry on; if it suggests a change of tack is needed then we change tack.

If the coachee feels a sense of progression , they are likely to succeed.

Finally

Build yourself a coaching question toolkit.

Write down as many questions you can think of that would be appropriate for each stage of the coaching process, the **G** the **R** the **O** and the **W**. Carry a notebook and whenever a good idea comes to you, write it down. Think of questions that may help break down limiting beliefs, challenging questions that might help break inertia and any other questions that you can think of. The purpose of this exercise is not to create a ready-made script but to train yourself into composing creative and proactive questions on the hoof when face to face with a coachee. The better the question the better the answer. Good answers produce better action plans which lead to better outcomes.

16 Postscript

Coaching skills are too good to be left solely for use of professional coaches; many people possess these skills and use them on a daily basis without ever consciously being aware of it. Somebody who is a good communicator is almost certainly using many of the skills and approaches; again, probably without knowing it.

Good communicators are good listeners, and so are good coaches. Active listening skills, the ability to take in and process and respond to what somebody has said, are an essential part of coaching. They are also key skills in being able to get on with our fellow workers, our friends and our family. The old adage that we have two ears and one mouth, so we should spend twice as much time listening as we do speaking, is good advice. It helps us understand what the other person is talking about as well as demonstrating to the person that we are really listening. This helps build rapport, which is always a good thing in any situation.

Many people who take coaching courses have no intention of becoming professional coaches, but intend to use the skills and knowledge acquired in their own work situations. Coaching skills are valuable in many different working environments, particularly where communication and staff encouragement are important parts of the ongoing daily business. Others take courses simply to be able to coach themselves and their family. Whatever the reasons, coaching skills can make us better communicators and listeners and, as a result, able to get on better with people in general.

Which surely cannot be a bad thing.

Now available in Spanish

**Una breve introducción
a las Habilidades de Coaching
y al Modelo GROW**

Translated from English by

Nicolas Argentato

www.modernforeignlanguages.net

Made in the USA
Las Vegas, NV
19 October 2022

57739730R00053